It's Rhode Island
A Cookbook
by Barbara Sherman Stetson

Author: Barbara Sherman Stetson
Illustrator: Marion King
Edited, Designed and Manufactured by:
Favorite Recipes® Press
an imprint of

P.O. Box 305142
Nashville, Tennessee 37230
1-800-358-0560

Library of Congress Catalog Number: 98-061540
ISBN: 0-9667034-0-5

Printed in the United States of America
First Printing: 1999

Introduction

It makes no difference whether you are a native of Rhode Island, a transplant, or a tourist, you'll love Rhode Island. There is always something to do—and especially something to eat!

Donna Lee, Food Editor of the *Providence Journal Bulletin,* has said to me, "Rhode Islanders have a passion for their food."

I hope that I have been able to capture some of that passion with some all-time-favorite and some new soon-to-become-favorite recipes. Some, as you would expect, feature seafood and other local products; some, the ethnic heritage of the area; and some the just plain wonderful food shared by families and restaurants throughout the state.

As the first of a new series called *It's America*

Cooking, it will bring you a taste of Rhode Island that is more than the food itself—a glimpse of the importance of food in the developing culture of Rhode Island since the days of Roger Williams, ethnic and religious influences, the fishing industry, agricultural products, festivals, events, and personalities that make Rhode Island unique.

If you enjoy this little book only half as much as I have while working on it—reliving fond memories, reveling in the present, and breaking bread while sharing friendships and experiences with others—that is what this book is about.

Please join me in the first step on what promises to be a richly fulfilling journey.

Barbara Sherman Stetson

Thank You

Thanks to all who have had the patience to put up with me, especially my artist and confidante, Marion King, to the owner of Herman's Hideaway, who is always there, Nancy, and the many contributors who have made this book what it is: Kathi Masi, Sigrid Bartel, Ethel and Bob Lambert, Colleen Lagueux, Jim Kirker, Sara Hutchings, Christina Dorr, "The Mayor," Shirley and Ed Hutchings, Leslie and Allan Olney, Sonia Welch, Tony Petrucci, Jane Folcarelli, Charlotte Blaine, the fine FRP staff (without whom there would be "No Book"), and Rhode Islanders all, for what they have contributed to the culture and diversity that is "Only in Rhode Island."

About the Artist

An artist of many talents, Marion King Wieselquist is well known in Rhode Island art circles. Her present career started after the birth of her son Erik. Born into a native Rhode Island family, she carries on the tradition of three generations of the noted King family.

Her outstanding wood carvings of birds and wildlife are second to none in the area. Collectors, not only in the New England area, but those fortunate enough to have visited the Cleveland Museum of Natural History and the American Museum of Natural History in New York, have viewed her works. A creative and original individual, Marion works in many media, including painting, illustrating, quilting, and other textile arts—as she says, "anything to avoid housework."

As an illustrator, she has *Receipts and Anecdotes of Scituate*, a 369-page cookbook by the Heritage Club, *A Cookbook of Swedish Memories* by Vivian Stenstrom, and, of course, *The Island Cookbook* by Barbara Sherman Stetson. Her love of cooking, the outdoors and things that "are real" are reflected in the realism and subtle humor of her work.

Table of Contents

Where Can I Find . . . ?

You may wish to visit some of the places mentioned in this book or perhaps purchase ingredients for recipes. This list should make your quest a little easier.

Carpenter's Grist Mill, 35 Narragansett Ave., Wakefield, RI 02879 (401/783-5483)

Federal Hill section of Providence, Atwells Avenue, Providence, RI

Gray's Grist Mill, P.O. Box 422, Adamsville, RI 02801 (508/636-6025)

Il Piccolo, 1450 Atwood Ave., Johnston, RI 02919 (401/421-9843)

Johnson & Wales University, College of Culinary Arts and Culinary Archives, Main Office, 8 Abbott Park Place, Providence, RI (401/598-1000)

Kenyon Corn Meal Co., Glen Rock Rd., Usquepaugh, RI 02892 (401/783-4054)

Market on the Boulevard, Memorial Blvd., Newport, RI 02840

Mayor's Own Marinara Sauce, Capital Innovations, Inc., 235 Promenade St., Providence, RI 02908

New Rivers American Bistro, 7 Steeple St., Providence, RI (401/751-0350)

Providence Journal Bulletin, 75 Fountain Street, Providence, RI 02903 (401/277-7000)

RIDEM, Div. of Agriculture, 83 Park St., Providence, RI 02903 (for listing of Rhode Island products, (401/277-2781)

Sakonnet Vineyards, P.O. Box 197, Little Compton, RI 02837 (401/635-2101)

To Kalon Club, 26 Main St., Pawtucket, RI (401/722-1310)

Touro Synagogue, 85 Touro St., Newport, RI 02840

Union Station Brewery, 38 Exchange St., Providence, RI (401/274-2739)

Westin Hotel, One West Exchange St., Providence, RI (401/598-8000)

Wickford Gourmet, 21 West Main St., Wickford, RI 02852 (401/295-8190)

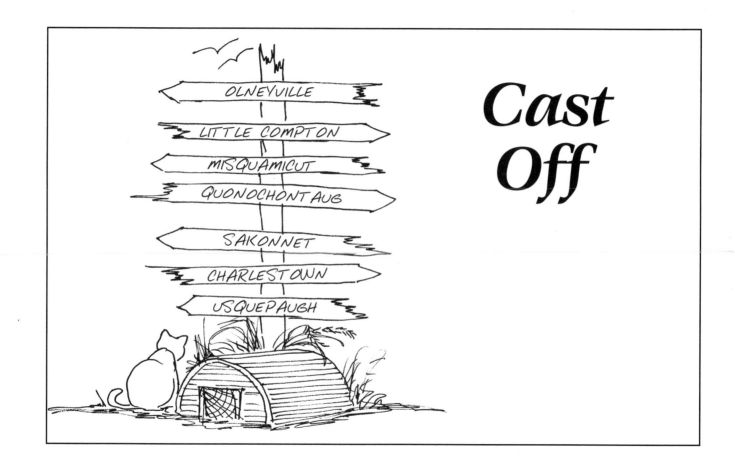

Portuguese Clam Dip

The Great Antipasto

So-Easy Pickled Beets

Marinated Mushrooms

Two Filo Appetizers

Baked Stuffed Quahogs

Bluefish Pâté

Pâte a Choux with Fillings

Stuffed Artichokes

Rhode Island Red Clam Chowder

Clamcakes

Smoked Salmon Spread

Neil's Seafood Bisque

Wedding Soup

Marion King's Corn Chowder

Bermuda Rarebit

Kathi's Broccoli Salad

Green Goddess Dressing

Angel Hair Pasta with Cilantro Vinaigrette

Basic Frittata

Comac Stew

Pepper and Egg Sandwich

Barbara's Favorite Jonnycake

Portuguese Clam Dip

A native of Portugal, Mary came to this country with a rare expertise in cooking. Known as the most wonderful cook in Weekapaug, she shares this creation with us.

4 cups chopped clams
Juice of ½ lemon
1 onion, minced
2 cloves of garlic, finely chopped
¼ cup olive oil
2 tablespoons unsalted butter
¼ large green bell pepper, finely chopped
¼ large red bell pepper, finely chopped
¼ cup chopped fresh parsley
½ teaspoon red pepper flakes
¼ teaspoon basil
7 slices fresh bread, crusts trimmed, dried
½ cup seasoned bread crumbs
½ teaspoon oregano
Freshly grated Parmesan cheese to taste
Paprika to taste
Butter to taste

❖ Drain the clams, reserving the juice. Mince the clams in a food processor. Combine with the reserved juice and lemon juice in a saucepan. Simmer for 5 minutes.

❖ Sauté the onion and garlic in the olive oil and 2 tablespoons butter in a large skillet until tender. Add bell peppers, parsley, pepper flakes and basil. Simmer for 5 minutes.

❖ Cut the bread into ½-inch squares. Mix the bread cubes, seasoned crumbs, oregano and clam mixture in the skillet. Add additional seasoned crumbs if necessary to make a paste consistency.

❖ Spoon into an ungreased 3-quart casserole. Sprinkle with Parmesan cheese and paprika.

❖ Bake at 350 degrees for 30 minutes or until bubbly. Dot with butter to prevent drying if necessary.

❖ Serve with low-salt wheat crackers. May freeze after baking. Thaw and microwave to rewarm.

The Great Antipasto

Is it the beginning, the middle, or the meal? we ask. Well, depending on your past experience, it can be any of those. Traditional Italian meals include a light green salad after the main course to cleanse the palate. As Italian foods became a favorite part of American cuisine, the salad became an introduction to the main course or sometimes an appetizer. The impatience of those who just couldn't wait for the main course to be served led to "we'll just have a little of this and a little of that" before the meal, and the antipasto became a first course. Believe it or not, the American custom of serving the salad before the main course moved from the West coast to the East.

An antipasto generally includes a variety of meats and vegetables—historically, the poorer the family, the less meat and cheese. Today, it may mean that someone is watching fat intake. Many different foods can be used in an antipasto, but the number and kinds are not so important as that they be attractively arranged on individual plates or on a large serving platter.

Salami, prosciutto, provolone or other cheeses,
Italian ham, celery, radishes, pickled beets, anchovies, black olives, hard-cooked eggs, marinated mushrooms, red peppers, stuffed tomatoes, artichoke hearts, tuna, pepperoni, scallions, and other assorted fresh vegetables all have a place. The presentation can be a simple or dramatic beginning for a meal or even the meal itself. Every family or restaurant has its own version.

An individual- or family-size antipasto starts with a loosely arranged bed of greens, and then anything goes—the only limitations are your budget, what is available and what you like. Here are two delicious additions to try on your personal antipasto.

So-Easy Pickled Beets

Adding cloves is especially good when the beets are to be served as an accompaniment with meat dishes.

1 (16-ounce) can sliced beets, drained
2 teaspoons sugar
Sliced onion to taste
1 teaspoon whole cloves (optional)
White or cider vinegar

- ❖ Combine the beets, sugar, onion and cloves in a bowl.

- ❖ Add enough vinegar to cover. Chill, covered, for 24 hours or longer.

Marinated Mushrooms

2 pounds fresh button mushrooms
$\frac{1}{2}$ cup white wine vinegar
1 envelope Italian salad dressing mix
$\frac{2}{3}$ cup cider vinegar
$\frac{1}{4}$ cup water
1 cup olive or canola oil
1 tablespoon sugar
2 cloves of garlic, minced
Tabasco sauce to taste

- ❖ Wipe the mushrooms with a damp paper towel. Remove the stems and chop the stems and caps into small pieces. Place the mushrooms in a saucepan and add the wine vinegar and enough water to cover. Boil for 3 minutes. Drain well.

- ❖ Mix the salad dressing mix, cider vinegar, $\frac{1}{4}$ cup water, olive oil, sugar, garlic and Tabasco sauce in a bowl.

- ❖ Add the hot mushrooms to the dressing and toss lightly. Cover and chill for 8 hours or longer before serving.

Two Filo Appetizers

Make these pretty and delicious appetizers ahead, store in the freezer, and then bake and serve whenever you wish. Once you learn to handle the filo with confidence, these will become a standby favorite.

Spinach and Cheese Appetizers

1 pound frozen filo dough
1 onion, finely minced
Olive oil
1 (10-ounce) package frozen chopped spinach, thawed
1/2 cup grated Parmesan cheese
8 ounces mozzarella cheese, finely diced
1 teaspoon chopped parsley
1 egg, slightly beaten
1/2 cup melted butter

❖ Thaw the filo according to the package directions.

❖ Sauté the onion in a small amount of olive oil in a large skillet.

❖ Drain the spinach and squeeze dry. Add the spinach, cheese and parsley to the skillet. Cook until dry, stirring frequently to mix well.

❖ Let the mixture cool. Mix in the egg.

❖ Cut the filo sheets lengthwise into thirds. Cover with a damp cloth or paper towel to prevent drying and cracking.

❖ Place 1 filo strip on work surface and brush with a small amount of melted butter. Place a teaspoon of spinach filling at one end of the filo strip and roll as for jelly roll. Place on a greased baking sheet. Repeat the process with the remaining ingredients.

❖ Keep appetizers covered with another damp cloth to prevent drying. (Appetizers may be frozen at this point and stored in plastic bags.)

❖ Remove the damp cloth. Bake at 350 degrees for 15 minutes. Serve hot.

❖ Yield: 45 appetizers.

Variations:

- ❖ Substitute desired amounts of minced garlic and shallots for the onion.

- ❖ Substitute minced artichoke hearts for the spinach.

Ham, Cheese and Eggplant Appetizers

1 pound frozen filo dough
8 ounces boiled ham, finely minced
8 ounces mozzarella cheese, finely diced
1 (4-ounce) jar pickled eggplant, drained, finely chopped
1 (3.5-ounce) can black olives, drained, finely chopped
¹/₂ cup melted butter

- ❖ Thaw the filo according to the package directions.

- ❖ Combine the ham, cheese, pickled eggplant and olives in a bowl and mix well.

- ❖ Cut the filo into strips and follow the directions above for assembling and baking the filo appetizers using the ham filling.

The REAL RHODE ISLAND is Aquidneck Island on the east side of Narragansett Bay, referred to by most tourists as Newport. The rest of the state is known as Providence Plantations, from the early days when the French occupied Newport and "the 400" summered in the cottages along Bellevue Drive and Ocean Drive. In the 1900s grand parties were given each season by the elite. Dinners included 12-course meals but were reduced to 6 for an elegant picnic under the elms. The elegance of bygone days is still alive and well—charity events, weddings, and the remaining few left of "the 400" see to it that the rich history of entertaining in the Newport area continues. Some of Rhode Island's finest restaurants have thrived in the Newport scene and are open year-round for those with a discerning palate.

Baked Stuffed Quahogs

There are as many variations of "Stuffies" as there are recipes. The Rhode Island fisherman who generously shared his version with us is noted for the best shellfish in Warwick. Use cherrystone clams for cocktail stuffies.

Andy's Stuffies

12 large quahogs, scrubbed
1 loaf day-old Italian bread, ground
1 egg, slightly beaten
1 green bell pepper, ground
1 medium onion, ground
1 clove of garlic, ground
1 tablespoon parsley flakes
$1/4$ teaspoon cayenne
3 tablespoons vegetable oil
1 (8-ounce) can tomato sauce
$1/4$ cup grated Parmesan cheese
Salt and black pepper to taste
Paprika to taste

❖ Place quahogs in a large kettle. Add 1 to 2 cups water. Bring to a boil. Steam, covered, until shells open.

❖ Drain, reserving liquid. Discard any unopened shells. Remove quahogs from shells; scrub shells inside and out. Grind quahogs.

❖ Mix bread with egg and enough reserved cooking liquid to soften.

❖ Sauté ground vegetables, parsley and cayenne in the oil in a large skillet until golden. Stir in the tomato sauce, quahogs, cheese, salt and black pepper. Simmer for 10 minutes. Add to the bread mixture and mix well.

❖ Spoon into quahog shells. Sprinkle with paprika. Place on a baking sheet. Bake at 400 degrees for 10 minutes. (Stuffies may be frozen before baking.)

14

"A Taste of Touro"

Roger Williams was not the only person to flee to Rhode Island to gain religious freedom. In 1658 Sephardim Jews of Spain and Portugal escaped from the Inquisition to Newport, Rhode Island. That congregation, now recognized as the earliest Jewish group in America, continued to grow. Today's Touro Synagogue still welcomes all to worship and share the belief that "freedom is the birthright of all men."

The Ladies Auxiliary of Congregation Jeshuat Israel created a cookbook in 1993 that is still available at Touro (see page 6.) One of Jack Temkin's favorite recipes is featured in the cookbook. It uses a fish that is native to Narragansett Bay. The recipe reminds me of good times shared with friends at Jewish celebrations. Bluefish and zucchini are probably Rhode Island's most prolific food products. Here is a delicious use for your extra blues.

The pâté is a wonderful addition to a cocktail menu that includes Filo Appetizers and Steak au Poivre. Serve with Sakonnet's America's Cup White or Pinot Noir and Cabernet Franc.

Bluefish Pâté

1 pound smoked bluefish
8 ounces unsalted butter, softened
8 ounces cream cheese, softened
1 small red onion, finely chopped
Juice of 1 lemon
1/4 teaspoon cayenne, or to taste
1/4 teaspoon white pepper
1/2 teaspoon salt
Dash of Worcestershire sauce
1/2 cup finely chopped fresh parsley
1/2 cup chopped pecans

❖ Remove bluefish skin; scrape off the dark fat.

❖ Combine the bluefish, butter, cream cheese, red onion, lemon juice, cayenne, white pepper, salt and Worcestershire sauce in a food processor or bowl. Mix until well blended. Chill for several hours.

❖ Shape into a log or ball. Roll in a mixture of parsley and pecans until well coated. Place on a serving plate. Garnish with parsley sprigs and serve with crackers.

Pâte a Choux

Better known as Puffs, these are a "must" for almost any occasion. Whether served as appetizer, dessert, or in lieu of a small sandwich, Puffs are quick, easy, and delightful.

Make Puffs ahead of time and freeze for later use. Freshen them with just 5 minutes in a 325-degree oven to crisp a little, fill with your favorite filling and replace the tops. "Keep an eye on them or they will burn," says Marion King.

The fillings can be made beforehand and refrigerated until ready to use. Do not fill the puffs until just before serving or they will become soggy, but remember to allow a little time for filling.

You can also use your favorite recipe for lobster, crab meat, tuna, or egg salad. Just be sure to chop all the ingredients finely enough to fill the puffs well.

Serve on glass dishes and garnish with flowering kale, parsley, or fresh edible flowers for a spectacular effect.

See page 67 for some Quick Dessert Puff ideas.

The Basic Puff

1 cup water
¹/₂ cup butter or margarine
¹/₄ teaspoon salt
1 cup flour
4 eggs, at room temperature

❖ Bring the water and butter to a full rolling boil in a large heavy saucepan. Add the salt and flour all at once. Stir vigorously with a wooden spoon until the mixture forms a ball. Remove from heat. Add the eggs 1 at a time, beating with an electric mixer after each addition until the mixture is thick and shiny.

❖ Fill a pastry bag with the mixture and pipe onto a baking sheet lined with parchment paper into quarter-size portions for miniature puffs or larger portions if desired.

❖ Bake small puffs at 400 degrees for 20 minutes or until light brown. Bake large puffs at 425 degrees for 15 minutes, reduce the oven temperature to 400 degrees and bake for 30 to 45 minutes longer or until light brown.

❖ Let the puffs stand in the oven with door ajar until cool. Cut the top from each puff just before serving using a serrated knife. Scoop out any slightly gooey center with a grapefruit spoon. Fill with your choice of filling.

❖ Yield: 45 miniature puffs or 8 to 10 large puffs.

Herbed Chicken Filling

1 whole chicken breast, cooked, minced
1 medium onion, minced
1 or 2 ribs celery, minced
$^1/_4$ teaspoon tarragon
$^1/_4$ teaspoon marjoram
$^1/_4$ teaspoon minced fresh parsley (optional)
$^3/_4$ to 1 cup mayonnaise
Salt and pepper to taste

❖ Combine the chicken, onion, celery, tarragon, marjoram and parsley in a bowl. Add enough mayonnaise to make the desired consistency. Add salt and pepper and mix well.

Variations:

❖ Add $^1/_4$ cup chopped walnuts or 1 finely chopped apple.

Ham Salad Filling

12 ounces ham
1 carrot, finely grated
$^1/_2$ green bell pepper, finely chopped (optional)
Chopped sweet pickle to taste
$^3/_4$ to 1 cup mayonnaise
$^1/_2$ teaspoon Dijon mustard

❖ Process the ham in a food processor until finely chopped. Add the remaining ingredients and mix lightly.

Cream Cheese and Olive Filling

8 ounces cream cheese, softened
$^1/_2$ cup minced pimento-stuffed green olives

❖ Mix the cream cheese with the olives.

A Food Editor and A Real Cook

When planning It's Rhode Island *I thought it was time that someone wrote about Donna Lee, Food Editor of the* Providence Journal Bulletin. *Her many and varied articles on new foods, food personalities— both national and local—and her excellent coverage of food news and events in the Rhode Island area all reflect what she calls "the passion Rhode Islanders have for fine food."*

After coming from the Midwest to work for the Boston Herald, *her introduction to the New England food industry was a whole new story.*

Some years ago she met her husband-to-be fter covering a food event at Johnson & Wales Culinary School, and later relocated to become the new guru of food in Rhode Island and Southern New England.

Well-respected in the world of journalism and food editing, Donna is also a wonderful cook. She reports that her style of cooking has changed in recent years.

Accustomed to cooking for a crowd, she now has learned to do the same as many of us: prepare for only two and adjust or restrict a few ingredients due to the need for healthy meals.

When I interviewed her, I inquired whether she really wanted me to reveal some of the things we had discussed over lunch. With a twinkle in her eye she said, "go ahead."

So here is the real scoop: Donna Lee doesn't use recipes for most of her favorite dishes—only when baking, she admitted. I agreed that I did the same but had to discipline myself to write down my recipes so other people could make them.

The most asked-for recipes from Donna are— believe it or not—Venus de Milo Soup and New York System Weiner Sauce. You will find the soup in The Island Cookbook *on page 37 and the Weiner Sauce in this book on page 37.*

Donna also shares with us her Stuffed Artichokes. According to Donna, in Italian households, stuffed artichokes are a popular treat at Easter—a fine first course before a rosemary-seasoned roast lamb. The peak season for artichokes is March through May.

Stuffed Artichokes

Serve also as delicious picnic fare with Antipasto, peasant bread, Lemon Ice Cream, Soft Molasses Cookies, and Sakonnet's Estate Chardonnay or Mariner Merlot or Union Station Ale.

4 fresh artichokes
1½ teaspoons minced garlic
1 to 2 tablespoons pignoli nuts (optional)
3 tablespoons olive oil
Crushed red pepper flakes to taste
1¼ cups Italian-seasoned bread crumbs
4 to 6 oil- or brine-cured black olives, chopped
2 tablespoons chopped fresh parsley or mint
2 tablespoons grated Romano or Parmesan cheese
5 tablespoons water or chicken broth
3 tablespoons olive oil
1 lemon wedge

❖ Trim 1 inch from the top of each artichoke and a thin slice from the stem end to form a base. Peel the stems and set aside. Boil the artichokes in a large kettle for 5 to 6 minutes or until the bases are fork-tender. Drain and cool. Spread the leaves; scrape out and discard the furry choke.

❖ Sauté the garlic and pignoli in 3 tablespoons olive oil in a large skillet until the garlic is tender but not brown. Add red pepper flakes and bread crumbs. Sauté until toasted. Add olives, parsley and cheese. Mix in the water.

❖ Place the artichokes in a baking dish. Spoon crumb mixture into centers and between leaves. Place reserved stems in center of stuffing. Drizzle 3 tablespoons olive oil over the top. Add the lemon wedge and a small amount of water to the baking dish. Bake, covered, at 350 degrees for 30 to 40 minutes or until a leaf can be pulled out easily.

Variations:

❖ Use unseasoned crumbs and add salt, pepper, basil or oregano to taste.

❖ Add chopped marinated sun-dried tomatoes to the crumbs.

Clamcakes and Chowder Rhode Island-Style

There is not only a controversy about jonnycakes, but about "chowda" as well. All types of clam chowder are served in the state but there are only two that are recognized as typical. Some purists insist that "broth chowder is real Rhode Island" and others that "red chowder is real Rhode Island." Both are made the same except that "red" has some type of tomato added.

Of course, in Rhode Island, most are made using quahogs, not clams, but you may substitute sea clams, minced clams, or canned clams if that is all you have available. If you don't have enough clam juice, use what you have with enough water added to measure 1 cup. Be aware that if quahogs or clams are cooked too long they will become tough.

To serve this recipe as broth chowder, omit the tomato and provide warm milk at the table for diners to add to their liking.

Rhode Island Red Clam Chowder

4 slices bacon, finely chopped
1 onion, minced
4 cups diced peeled potatoes
1 cup clam juice
2 cups boiling water
1 cup strained stewed tomatoes or 1 cup tomato soup
2 cups chopped clams or quahogs
Salt and pepper to taste

❖ Fry the bacon in a heavy saucepan until crisp and brown. Remove and reserve the bacon. Add the onion. Sauté until transparent.

❖ Add the potatoes, clam juice and boiling water. Simmer until almost tender.

❖ Add the tomatoes and clams. Cook for about 5 minutes. Add salt and pepper.

❖ Ladle into bowls. Garnish with reserved bacon. Serve with oyster crackers or clamcakes.

Clamcakes

Clamcakes are not fritters or pancakes. This is a typical recipe, but if you would prefer using a mix there are several at local markets. Look for Krispee, Carpenter's, Gray's, or Kenyon's.

1 cup flour
1 teaspoon baking powder
$1/8$ teaspoon salt
Dash of pepper
$2/3$ cup clam juice
1 egg, beaten
1 (12-ounce) can chopped clams, drained
Vegetable oil for deep-frying

❖ Combine the flour, baking powder, salt and pepper in a bowl. Mix in the clam juice, egg and clams. Batter should not be runny so add a small amount of additional flour if necessary.

❖ Preheat the oil to 375 degrees. Drop the batter by teaspoonfuls into the hot oil. Deep-fry until light brown, turning once. Drain on paper towels and serve hot.

Smoked Salmon Spread

Those who prefer a low-fat appetizer will find this spread a seaworthy alternative.

1 slice smoked salmon, finely chopped
3 tablespoons minced onion
8 ounces nonfat cottage cheese
Dash of pepper
Red radish and green bell pepper slices

❖ Combine the salmon, onion, cottage cheese and pepper in a bowl and mix well. Chill until serving time. Spoon into a serving bowl or onto a serving plate. Garnish with radish and green pepper slices and serve with crackers.

The To Kalon Club

The Club was established in 1867 by Pawtucket industrialists and businessmen as a place where gentlemen could have a decent lunch or dinner and not be interrupted. The words "To Kalon" are from the Greek and mean good, beautiful hospitality. My husband was a member and enjoyed it thoroughly.

The only problem I found with the club was the limited access to women. Until 1966 women were admitted for specific functions only. In 1990, as guests of a member, women could gain access to the dining room, and finally, in 1994, women could become members. I still fondly call the TK Club "the pig club," much to the chagrin of the manager. It certainly does not deserve that name now that it has come into the twenty-first century while keeping the ambiance and charm of the olden days.

It is available for intimate weddings, prenuptial dinners, bridal showers, and bachelor parties. A billiard room, card room, and four-lane bowling alley are available. No matter the need, from luncheon to special event, the food and service are superb.

Probably one of the easiest recipes in the book, this quick first course from Chef Neil Chandley was pronounced "a must" by Donna Lee, Food Editor of the Providence Journal Bulletin. We have adapted it for you in a smaller quantity than Neil makes for the members.

Neil grew up working in his family's restaurant in Massachusetts learning how to make everything from soup to nuts. He obviously learned his lessons well.

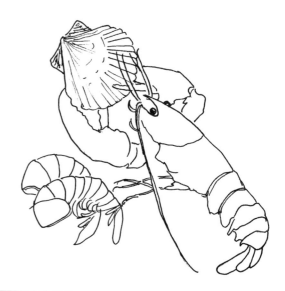

Neil's Seafood Bisque

1 pound unpeeled shrimp
1 pound scallops
8 cups water
2 seafood bouillon cubes
$^1/_2$ cup butter
6 tablespoons flour
1 teaspoon Worcestershire sauce
3 to 6 shakes Tabasco sauce
$^1/_2$ teaspoon garlic powder
$^1/_4$ teaspoon white pepper
Salt to taste
$1^1/_4$ to $1^1/_2$ cups half-and-half
Fresh or dried dill to taste

❖ Place the shrimp and scallops in a 4- to 5-quart soup pot. Add water and bouillon cubes. Bring to a simmer. Simmer for 5 minutes. Remove the shrimp and scallops. Set the broth aside.

❖ Peel the shrimp. Set shrimp and scallops aside.

❖ Melt the butter in a heavy pan. Add the flour and blend well. Cook over low heat for 3 to 4 minutes, stirring constantly. Set aside.

❖ Process half the shellfish in a food processor until minced and set aside. Process the remaining shellfish until very finely minced. Add the shellfish, Worcestershire sauce, Tabasco sauce, garlic powder, pepper and salt to the soup pot. Simmer for 5 minutes. Adjust seasonings.

❖ Whisk in the roux. Simmer for 5 minutes, whisking frequently. Stir in half-and-half. Heat to serving temperature; DO NOT BOIL.

❖ Serve in hot mugs or soup bowls with a light sprinkle of dill.

❖ Note: Bisque may be frozen in pint containers before adding the half-and-half.

Variations:

❖ Make a reduced-fat version for those watching their fat intake by substituting evaporated skim milk for the half-and-half.

❖ Substitute lobster or crab meat or other seafood mixture for the scallops and shrimp.

Is It Soup Yet?

Traditionally, many Rhode Island wedding dinners begin with a light chicken soup served family-style. Sometimes called escarole soup, it is served at holidays or as a family meal with salad and crisp Italian bread.

Wedding Soup

1½ **pounds chicken pieces**
1 **carrot, finely chopped**
1 **onion, finely chopped**
1 **rib celery, finely chopped**
1 **or 2 chicken bouillon cubes (optional)**
Salt and pepper to taste
8 **ounces extra-lean ground beef**
1 **head escarole, cleaned, chopped**
½ **cup uncooked orzo**
Sliced hard-boiled eggs

❖ Combine the chicken, carrot, onion, celery and bouillon cubes in a large soup pot. Add water to cover, salt and pepper. Simmer for 30 to 40 minutes or until the chicken is tender.

❖ Remove the chicken, discard skin and bones and cut into ½-inch cubes. Return to the broth.

❖ Shape ground beef into tiny meatballs. Add to the broth with escarole. Simmer for 15 minutes.

❖ Cook the orzo using package directions for 5 minutes. Drain and add to the soup.

❖ Garnish with hard-boiled eggs. Serve with Parmesan cheese at the table.

Reduced-Calorie Wedding Soup

❖ Omit the chicken and onion. Cook the carrot and celery in a 48-ounce can of low-fat chicken broth mixed with 2 cups water for 10 minutes. Add ½ head escarole and 4 ounces ground beef shaped into tiny meatballs; cook for 10 to 12 minutes.

Marion King's Corn Chowder

4 slices bacon, finely chopped
1/2 large sweet onion, finely chopped
2 ribs celery, finely chopped
2 (16-ounce) cans chicken broth
1 carrot, finely chopped
4 to 6 medium potatoes, peeled, chopped
1 (16-ounce) can cream-style corn
1/2 teaspoon salt
Pepper to taste
1 cup warm milk
1/4 teaspoon each minced fresh marjoram, dill, thyme and parsley

❖ Sauté the bacon in a saucepan. Reserve bacon. Sauté the onion and celery in bacon drippings. Add broth, carrot, potatoes, corn, salt and pepper. Simmer until the potatoes are almost tender.

❖ Add the milk. Simmer until the potatoes are tender. Top with bacon and herbs.

Bermuda Rarebit

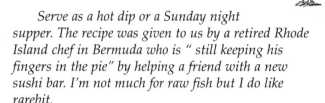

Serve as a hot dip or a Sunday night supper. The recipe was given to us by a retired Rhode Island chef in Bermuda who is " still keeping his fingers in the pie" by helping a friend with a new sushi bar. I'm not much for raw fish but I do like rarebit.

1/2 cup beer
1 pound extra-sharp Cheddar cheese, shredded
1 or 2 dashes of paprika
2 teaspoons Sherry Pepper Sauce (optional)
4 to 6 slices French bread

❖ Heat the beer in a double boiler over hot water. Add the cheese and paprika. Heat until the cheese melts, stirring occasionally.

❖ Add pepper sauce just before serving. Serve with the French bread.

Kathi's Broccoli Salad

Serve this quick, easy, colorful salad with any seafood dish or other entrée.

1 large head broccoli, or 4 (10-ounce) packages frozen broccoli spears, thawed
1 (4-ounce) jar roasted red bell pepper or 1 red bell pepper, thinly sliced
2 cloves of garlic, minced
Juice of 1 lemon
2 to 4 tablespoons olive oil
Cracked black peppercorns to taste
1 lemon, thinly sliced

❖ Trim the broccoli, leaving about 2 inches of stalk. Blanch in lightly salted water for 3 minutes. Drain, cool quickly on shaved ice and drain well. Place on serving platter. Cut roasted pepper into thin strips and place between broccoli spears. Cover with plastic wrap.

❖ Whisk garlic, lemon juice, olive oil and pepper together. Drizzle over salad. Top with lemon slices. Serve chilled or at room temperature.

Green Goddess Dressing

Once very popular and frequently used as an ingredient in other recipes, this dressing is now hard to find in supermarkets. Here is an updated version. Use it on greens of any kind but especially over romaine and garnished with croutons. Try it as a dip with fresh vegetables or crackers.

1/2 cup minced black olives
3 tablespoons anchovy paste
1/3 cup finely minced onion
1 cup fat-free mayonnaise
2/3 cup evaporated skim milk
2 tablespoons lemon juice
1/4 cup tarragon vinegar
1/4 cup minced parsley
Garlic powder, salt and pepper to taste

❖ Mix olives and anchovy paste in a medium bowl. Mix in the remaining ingredients. Adjust the seasonings. Chill for several hours.

❖ Yield: 2³/₄ cups.

A New Look for Pasta in Providence

The Keep Providence Beautiful Pasta Challenge is held every fall. As a judge, I felt it important that "white" have a place and that angel hair be recognized as a bonafide salad ingredient. The culinary staff of the Westin Hotel, Providence, has designed this wonderful summer salad with delightful full-bodied flavor and crunch. All the vegetables should be a fine julienne.

Cilantro Vinaigrette

$1/2$ cup olive oil
$1/4$ cup fresh lemon juice
2 tablespoons white wine vinegar
2 tablespoons Dijon mustard
3 large cloves of garlic, minced
$1/2$ cup chopped cilantro
Salt and pepper to taste

❖ Whisk all ingredients in a bowl. Chill.

Angel Hair Pasta with Cilantro Vinaigrette

$1^1/_2$ pounds angel hair pasta
1 summer squash, julienned
1 zucchini, julienned
1 medium carrot, julienned
$1/2$ Daikon radish, julienned
1 medium red onion, julienned
2 large roasted red bell peppers, julienned
1 large tomato, julienned
Cilantro Vinaigrette

❖ Cook the angel hair pasta according to the package directions, drain and cool.

❖ Blanch the squash, zucchini, carrot and radish in boiling water for 3 minutes; drain and cool.

❖ Add to the angel hair pasta with the remaining vegetables.

❖ Add the Cilantro Vinaigrette, toss to mix and chill until serving time.

Brown Eggs

Eggs in New England are, of course, brown, particularly in Rhode Island, the birthplace of the Rhode Island Red chicken. As the commercials on television and radio proudly announce, "Brown eggs are local eggs and local eggs are fresh." White eggs are available at Easter in abundance, but not during the rest of the year.

This popular lunch, brunch, or supper dish traces its heritage from Italian and Portuguese cooking. Start with this basic recipe and vary with your own favorite ingredients.

Basic Frittata

1 onion, finely chopped
2 tablespoons olive oil
3 or 4 boiled or baked potatoes, thinly sliced or
   cut into 1-inch cubes
6 to 8 eggs, well beaten
2 to 3 tablespoons water

❖ Sauté the onion in olive oil in a 10- to 12-inch skillet until partially cooked. Add the potatoes and mix lightly.

❖ Beat the eggs with the water. Pour over the potato mixture. Cook over medium heat, lifting the edges slightly to allow uncooked egg to flow to the bottom of the skillet.

❖ Turn over when the eggs are set. (Cut the frittata into halves for easier turning or invert onto a hot lightly oiled skillet of the same size.) Cook for 1 to 2 minutes longer.

Variations:

❖ Add sliced or shredded zucchini to the potatoes.

❖ Substitute chopped tomatoes and zucchini for the potatoes.

❖ Add chopped ham, chourico or green bell pepper.

Comac Stew

This old Yankee receipt is still easy, inexpensive, and tasty today. Add ¼ cup shredded sharp cheese or season with tarragon or dill for variety. Egg substitute works well, too.

1 small onion, chopped
1 teaspoon margarine
2 cups chopped tomatoes
Salt and pepper to taste
2 eggs

❖ Sauté the onion in margarine in a skillet until tender. Add the tomatoes. Cook for 5 to 10 minutes, stirring frequently. Sprinkle with salt and pepper to taste.

❖ Beat the eggs with a fork until fluffy. Pour the eggs into the vegetable mixture. Cook until the eggs are set, stirring gently. Serve on toast.

Pepper and Egg Sandwich

Jealousy reared its ugly head when I reached fifth grade. I was used to peanut butter and jelly, bologna and mustard or maybe a meat loaf sandwich, and could hardly believe my eyes when I saw classmates with wonderful torpedo rolls or Italian bread wrapped around an omelet and called a "pepper and egg sangwich." After a few months, I got up enough courage to ask a classmate if I could try this extraordinary looking concoction. I did, and thought I had died and gone to heaven. Even now, it is a treat.

1 large green bell pepper, seeded, sliced, cut up
Olive oil to taste
4 eggs, beaten
Salt and pepper to taste
2 torpedo rolls

❖ Sauté the green pepper in olive oil until tender. Pour in the eggs. Cook over medium heat for 3 minutes or until set but not dry, lifting the edges slightly to allow egg to flow to the bottom of the skillet. Sprinkle with salt and pepper. Place in the rolls. Serve hot or cold.

Jonnycakes Are Not Hush Puppies

Although served in much the same way, their origin is different and so is the recipe. It is believed that the Rhode Island Jonnycake started off as a journeycake in a hat, became a jarneycake, and eventually a jonnycake or johnnycake. They are all made much alike, but not the same as the johnnycake of the Midwest or New Hampshire, and are fried and not baked or baked and then fried. Are you confused? Depending on your Rhode Island heritage or location, another controversy exists. Do you like them thick as in South County or thin as in Newport County? Served with maple syrup and butter or creamed dried beef? Enjoy them all—the key word is "delicious."

A hint for those who have never made jonnycakes successfully: You probably have not used boiling water, not added the water all at once, or not beaten the mixture well. All the steps need to be done correctly, so the cornmeal is scalded and will swell and absorb the water. This prevents a raw taste even after the jonnycake is fried.

Barbara's Favorite Jonnycake

Neither thick nor thin—just right!

1 cup stone-ground white cornmeal
1/4 teaspoon salt
2 teaspoons sugar
1 1/2 cups (about) boiling water
Milk
Bacon drippings or shortening

❖ Mix the cornmeal, salt and sugar in a bowl. Add the boiling water all at once, mixing until blended. If batter is too thick, stir in small amounts of milk.

❖ Drop by tablespoonfuls onto a well greased 375-degree griddle or a very heavy pan that heats evenly. (My grandmother always used a spider.) Use enough drippings or shortening. The secret in dropping the batter is in the wrist. Cook for 5 to 6 minutes; do not pat or play with the batter. Turn over when the edges are brown and cook until light brown. Serve immediately.

Steak au Poivre

Woonsocket Meat Pie

The New York System Hot Weiner Sauce

Boneless Pork Loin with Herb Crust

Wayne's Orzo

Carrots l'Orange

Roast Loin of Pork with Bourbon Gravy

Country Sausage and Beef Casserole

Wild Mushroom Polenta with Mushroom
and Tomato Gravy

Grilled Portobello Mushrooms

Chicken Penne

Pollo Fantasia con Vegetali

Marion King's Studio Casserole

Kirk's Spinach Flounder

Swordfish Westerly

Herb Butter for Baked or Broiled Swordfish

Block Island Scalloped Lobster

Rhode Island Baked Stuffed Shrimp

Special from Herman's Hideaway

Some of you may remember the story of Herman's Hideaway from The Island Cookbook. *Whenever my husband, Carl, decided we should have a special meal, he would always cook, and I, fortunately, would be invited to "his restaurant." This is a recipe that he adapted from a dish he had enjoyed while on a business trip to New York.*

To serve as an appetizer, cut the steak into 1-inch strips before cooking. Proceed as the recipe directs and serve from a chafing dish. Don't forget to provide sturdy toothpicks or small forks for your guests.

Whether you decide to use this recipe as an appetizer or an entrée, your guests will rave over how tasty the meat is!

The secret is in selecting the right cut of beef. This recipe demands flavorful, tender steak such as sirloin or strip loin, cut 1^1/$_2$ inches thick.

Steak au Poivre

2^1/$_2$ **pounds steak, trimmed**
Salt to taste
3 tablespoons whole black peppercorns
^{1}/$_4$ **cup olive oil**
^{1}/$_4$ **cup brandy**
1 cup half-and-half

❖ Score the steak edges. Salt on both sides.

❖ Crush peppercorns coarsely in a folded clean dry towel with a rolling pin or skillet. Press the pepper evenly over both sides of the steak.

❖ Pan-broil the steak in the olive oil in a very hot skillet. Remove to a warm platter. Keep warm in a 325-degree oven.

❖ Flame 1 tablespoon of the pan drippings with the brandy for 1 minute. Add the half-and-half. Heat until thickened, stirring constantly. Pour over steak. Garnish with chopped fresh parsley. Serve with rice pilaf and green vegetables.

❖ Yield: 4 servings.

In the City of Woonsocket

French Canadians migrated in large numbers to the northernmost Rhode Island city of Woonsocket. Many were hardworking millworkers with large families who brought with them traditional recipes. Probably the one that is most enjoyed by Rhode Islanders is the French Meat Pie that is always served on New Year's Eve, while the English claim fame in parts of Rhode Island to Hartley's Pork Pies. Here is the Woonsocket version for you to try.

There are two different seasoning mixes that may be used to make the pie. Try each of the mixes to choose your favorite.

The Woonsocket Meat Pie makes a wonderfully hearty addition to a buffet table stocked with Seafood Bisque, Chicken Penne, Broccoli Salad, Angel Hair Pasta with Cilantro Vinaigrette, Squash Biscuits, Margot's Cheesecake and served with Sakonnet's Vidal Blanc, Cabernet Franc and America's Cup White.

Woonsocket Meat Pie

1 pound lean ground beef
1 pound ground pork
1 large onion, finely chopped
1 cup water
Seasoning Mix I or Seasoning Mix II (page 35)
2 potatoes, peeled, cooked, mashed
Saltine crackers to taste
Pie Pastry
1 egg, beaten

❖ Crumble the ground beef and ground pork into a large skillet. Add the onion and water and mix well. Mix in your choice of seasoning mix.

❖ Simmer, uncovered, for 30 minutes, stirring occasionally.

❖ Add the mashed potatoes and mix well. Crush some crackers and stir into the meat mixture until the filling is of the desired consistency.

- Spoon the filling into the pastry-lined pie plate. Top with the remaining pastry, sealing the edge and cutting vents.

- Beat the egg with a small amount of cold water to make an egg wash. Brush evenly over the top pastry.

- Bake at 425 degrees for 10 minutes. Reduce the oven temperature to 350 degrees. Bake for 30 minutes longer or until the crust is golden brown.

- Let stand for several minutes. Cut into wedges. Serve with catsup.

Seasoning Mix I:

- Combine 1 to 2 tablespoons poultry seasoning with $^1/_4$ teaspoon salt and $^1/_8$ teaspoon pepper.

Seasoning Mix II:

- Combine $^1/_4$ teaspoon each ground cloves and cinnamon with $^1/_4$ teaspoon dried marjoram and salt and pepper to taste.

Pie Pastry

4 cups flour
1 tablespoon sugar
1$^1/_2$ teaspoons salt
1$^3/_4$ cups shortening
1 egg, beaten
$^1/_2$ cup water
1 teaspoon vinegar

- Combine the flour, sugar and salt in a bowl and mix well. Cut in the shortening with a pastry blender or two knives until the mixture is crumbly.

- Beat the egg with water and vinegar. Pour into the flour mixture and mix with a fork until the mixture holds together. Shape into a ball and wrap in plastic wrap. Chill for 1 hour or freeze for future use.

- Divide the dough into 2 equal portions. Roll on a lightly floured surface. Fit 1 portion into a 9- or 10-inch pie plate. Keep the remaining pastry covered to prevent drying.

The New York System Hot Weiner

If you are from out-of-state, you may want to sample a New York System Hot Weiner before you attempt to make them. Your frame of mind as you try them may make all the difference.

My first encounter with the weiners and their famous sauce took place in the Olneyville district of Providence. The place was Handlebar Mike's, where the dish is known as the Olneyville New York System. Visitors may be treated to the not unusual sight of fifteen or more buns with weiners propped upon the proprietor's arm. The weiners may be dressed with only the special weiner sauce or "all the way," which includes the sauce, mustard, chopped onion and, celery salt.

The weiners themselves are produced locally in long strings that are cut apart to more or less fit the buns, which are always steamed — not grilled or toasted.

Donna Lee, Food Editor of the Providence Journal, says that the recipe most often requested from her is for New York Hot Weiner Sauce. Here are two versions for you to try.

The first version is an adaption of a recipe from the former Royal Lunch in Hoyle Square. I happened by the recipe because a friend of mine used to work there. When the owner of the establishment had to go to the hospital many years ago, the secret recipe was given to a trusted employee named Tony.

When Tony was moving to a new home last year he found a scrap of paper with that recipe in his belongings. He shared it with me. After being lost for 40 years, the secret is now out!

Of course the amounts had to be reduced — the original recipe took 30 pounds of ground beef and 6 ladles of chili powder. After much testing and tasting by local afficionados of New York System Hot Weiners, here it is!

Rhode Island-Style Hot Weiner Sauce

1¹/₂ pounds lean ground beef
4 ounces bacon, minced
1 large onion, minced
¹/₂ large green bell pepper, minced
3 large cloves of garlic, minced
1¹/₂ teaspoons nutmeg
2 teaspoons paprika
1 teaspoon sugar
¹/₂ (6-ounce) can tomato paste
¹/₂ cup water

❖ Process the ground beef in a food processor until very fine and set aside.

❖ Cook the bacon in a heavy skillet or Dutch oven until crisp. Add the onion, green pepper and garlic. Sauté until tender and light brown.

❖ Add the ground beef. Cook until crumbly, stirring frequently. Stir in the remaining ingredients. Cook over low heat for 2 to 3 hours, stirring occasionally.

❖ Cool and store in airtight containers in the freezer.

Another Weiner Sauce

As with the first version, the ground beef needs to be very fine so be sure that it is ground twice. The finished consistency should be like chili.

1¹/₂ pounds lean ground beef
¹/₂ cup chopped onion
1¹/₄ teaspoons each ground cumin and paprika
¹/₄ teaspoon each celery salt and allspice
1 teaspoon salt
1 teaspoon prepared mustard
1 tablespoon chili powder
2¹/₂ cups water

❖ Crumble the ground beef into a heavy skillet. Add the onion, seasonings and water.

❖ Bring to a simmer, stirring frequently. Simmer, loosely covered, for 45 minutes, stirring occasionally and adding water if necessary.

The National High School Recipe Contest

Sponsored by Johnson & Wales University of Providence, the American Heart Association, and the American Cancer Society, this contest provides a forum for young people to compete creatively and win scholarships to be used in culinary training.

Johnson & Wales started as a small business school but has grown to be one of the largest culinary schools in the world. Many chefs of national reputation started there.

A recent grand prize winner was Wayne King of Montauk, New York, for his entry, Orzo-Stuffed Pork Tenderloin with Herb Crust. As one of his judges, I have taken the liberty of simplifying his recipe somewhat.

Serve this extraordinary recipe with Sakonnet's Pinot Noir or Fumé Vidal.

Boneless Pork Loin with Herb Crust

¹/₄ cup minced fresh rosemary
3 tablespoons dried thyme
Freshly ground pepper to taste
1 teaspoon salt
1 tablespoon poultry seasoning
1 (4- to 5-pound) boneless pork loin
1 cup chicken broth

❖ Mix the rosemary, thyme, pepper, salt and poultry seasoning on waxed paper. Place the pork loin on the waxed paper and roll in the herb mixture until coated. Place the coated pork in a roasting pan and add 1 inch of water.

❖ Roast, covered, at 350 degrees for 20 to 25 minutes per pound to 160 degrees on a meat thermometer or 170 degrees for well done. Check during the roasting time and add additional water to prevent cooking dry.

❖ Remove the pork to a platter. Deglaze the pan with the broth. Serve the juices with the pork.

Wayne's Orzo

Wayne stuffed his pork tenderloin with the orzo mixture and you can certainly do that with the boneless pork loin if you wish, but I suggest for those who are timid with new practices that the orzo be served as a side dish. The orzo may be prepared beforehand and then reheated in the oven or microwaved at serving time.

3 cups canned chicken broth
1 cup orzo
$1/2$ cup chopped shallots
1 cup finely chopped carrots
1 cup finely chopped celery
2 tablespoons olive oil
2 tablespoons butter
$1/4$ cup minced Italian parsley
6 tablespoons Parmesan cheese
Salt and freshly ground pepper to taste

❖ Bring the chicken broth to a boil in a medium saucepan. Add the orzo. Cook for 7 to 8 minutes or until all the broth is absorbed, stirring frequently.

❖ Sauté the shallots, carrots and celery in the olive oil and butter in a large saucepan until tender. Add the cooked orzo and mix well. Stir in the parsley, Parmesan cheese, salt and pepper.

❖ Spoon the mixture into a serving bowl or use to stuff the pork before roasting.

Carrots l'Orange

1 pound carrots, peeled, sliced
Juice and zest of 1 orange
$1/2$ teaspoon dried tarragon
Salt to taste
1 tablespoon butter or margarine

❖ Combine all ingredients in a saucepan. Add just enough water to cover. Cook, covered, for 15 minutes or until tender. Drain, reserving the cooking liquid. Keep the carrots warm.

❖ Cook the reserved liquid over medium heat until reduced to the desired amount and consistency. Serve over the carrots.

Roast Loin of Pork with Bourbon Gravy

Rhode Island has not only a wealth of outstanding restaurants, but outstanding food selections from local markets and specialty stores. This Christmas holiday special is from the Village IGA in North Scituate.

3 tablespoons olive oil
1 teaspoon dried thyme leaves, crumbled
1 teaspoon dried oregano leaves, crumbled
1 tablespoon caraway seeds
1 teaspoon coarse salt
1 small onion, finely chopped
1 teaspoon crushed fresh garlic
1 (4- to 5-pound) pork loin, boneless or bone-in with split chine bone
1 cup chicken broth
2 tablespoons bourbon (optional)
3/4 cup water
1 1/2 tablespoons cornstarch
1/2 cup cold water
1/2 cup chopped green onions, or 1/4 cup chopped chives

❖ Combine the olive oil, thyme, oregano, caraway seeds, salt, onion and garlic in a small bowl and mix well. Rub the mixture over all surfaces of the pork. Refrigerate, tightly covered, for 6 to 8 hours or longer.

❖ Place the pork in a roasting pan. Roast, uncovered, at 350 degrees for 1 hour or to 155 degrees on a meat thermometer.

❖ Remove the pork to a platter. Cover loosely with foil. Deglaze the roasting pan with broth, bourbon and 3/4 cup water, scraping the bottom and sides of the pan well. Bring to a boil.

❖ Dissolve the cornstarch in the cold water. Stir into the roasting pan. Cook over low heat for 2 to 3 minutes, stirring constantly.

❖ Cut the pork into 1/2- to 3/4-inch slices. Place on plates. Top with a small amount of the gravy. Sprinkle with the green onions. Add a garnish of pickled crabapples. Serve the remaining gravy in a gravy boat at the table.

❖ Yield: 6 to 8 servings.

Country Sausage and Beef Casserole

A popular family recipe for a hearty supper or an outdoor picnic, this easy-to-prepare dish can be made beforehand and reheated. It is a favorite dish at Preservation Society potluck suppers.

1 pound hot or sweet Italian sausage
1 pound stew beef or round, cut into 1-inch
   cubes
1 large onion, sliced
3 medium cloves of garlic, minced
2 green bell peppers, cut into 1-inch pieces
5 medium potatoes, quartered
1 (16-ounce) can water-pack red kidney beans
1 (16-ounce) can stewed tomatoes
1 teaspoon sweet basil
$1/2$ teaspoon salt
$1/4$ teaspoon pepper
2 beef bouillon cubes
1 cup boiling water

❖ Cut each sausage link into thirds or smaller pieces. Cook in a heavy skillet over medium heat until brown on all sides. Place the sausage in a 3-quart baking dish. Pour most of the drippings from the skillet.

❖ Cook the beef cubes in the remaining drippings in the skillet until brown on all sides. Place in the baking dish.

❖ Add the onion, garlic and peppers to the skillet. Sauté for 2 minutes or until partially cooked. Add to the baking dish.

❖ Add the potatoes, beans, tomatoes, basil, salt and pepper to the baking dish and mix well.

❖ Dissolve the bouillon cubes in the boiling water. Pour into the baking dish.

❖ Bake, covered, at 350 degrees for $1^{1}/2$ hours or until the beef and potatoes are tender.

❖ Serve with a green salad, crusty bread and Sakonnet's Rhode Island Red wine.

❖ Yield: 6 to 8 servings.

PROVIDENCE *is a city of many faces and home to some of the finest schools in the country—Brown University, Providence College, Rhode Island School of Design, University of Rhode Island, Rhode Island College, Roger Williams University, and Johnson & Wales University.*

There is much to do and see in Providence and neighboring communities, with wonderful museums of every type, architecture from the 1700s, an ever-changing waterfront, and the State House with the fourth-largest dome of its type in the world. And, of course, restaurants that are known all over the country for their pizazz and tip-top menus.

New Rivers

When New Rivers is mentioned in Providence or in tourist information, it generally refers to the undertaking of the City of Providence to relocate two rivers, the Woonasquatucket and Moshassuck, which flow through the city. This project was the beginning of Providence being known as "a Renaissance city."

In this book, New Rivers is a success story about a young couple who graduated from college, one in Rhode Island, the other in California, who met in Lake Tahoe and became working partners in New England. They married and attended Madeleine Kamman's Boston Cooking School.

After several interesting jobs, Pat and Bruce Tillinghast established New Rivers in 1990. This American bistro is one of the hidden treasures of Rhode Island. The ambiance of the site is a 1793 warehouse between North Main and Canal streets at the foot of College Hill, only a ten-minute walk from the Westin Hotel, the Rhode Island Convention Center and "Waterfire."

Bruce says they like to feature local food products in season and keep things interesting by changing the menu five or six times a year to celebrate the cuisine of ethnic and cultural groups.

I was able to convince him to share one of my favorite dishes from his menu. He insisted that it was too time-consuming for most cooks, but I feel that it is well worth it.

If you don't wish to make your own polenta, you may purchase it ready-made, but it won't be like this.

Wild Mushroom Polenta with Mushroom and Tomato Sauce

The stone-ground cornmeal for this recipe is especially milled for New Rivers by Gray's Grist Mill.

1/2 ounce dried porcini mushrooms
3/4 cup hot water
1 tablespoon minced garlic
1 tablespoon minced shallots
1 cup chopped onion
1/2 cup chopped crimini mushrooms
1 1/2 teaspoons dried thyme
1 1/2 teaspoons dried rosemary
4 cups water
1 vegetable bouillon cube
1 1/2 cups coarsely ground cornmeal
1/2 cup grated Asiago cheese
Cream
Wild Mushroom and Tomato Sauce (page 44)
Grilled Portobello Mushrooms (page 44)
Fontina cheese

❖ Soak the porcini mushrooms in the hot water for 30 minutes.

❖ Sauté the garlic, shallots, onion and crimini mushrooms in a heavy saucepan until the onion is translucent. Add herbs. Sauté for several minutes longer.

❖ Pour the water from the porcini mushrooms and 4 cups water into the saucepan. Add chopped mushrooms to the saucepan. Bring to a boil, add the bouillon cube and stir until dissolved.

❖ Stir in the cornmeal gradually. Cook for 1 minute, stirring constantly. Reduce the heat to low. Cook for 30 minutes, stirring frequently to prevent sticking.

❖ Stir in the cheese. Spread in an oiled 8-inch-square pan to cool. Cut into 6 squares when set.

❖ Place the polenta in a shallow baking dish. Circle with a small amount of cream and Wild Mushroom and Tomato Sauce. Top with sliced Grilled Portobello Mushrooms, Mushroom and Tomato Sauce, a thin slice of fontina cheese and additional Asiago cheese. Bake at 450 degrees for 8 to 10 minutes or until bubbly.

Wild Mushroom and Tomato Sauce

You may use your favorite sauce, adding 2 ounces of dried porcini mushrooms, or a purchased sauce.

2 ounces dried porcini mushrooms
2 cups hot water
1/4 cup minced shallots
2 tablespoons olive oil
6 tablespoons butter
3 1/2 cups puréed canned tomatoes
1 1/2 teaspoons each dried rosemary and thyme
Salt and pepper to taste

❖ Soak the mushrooms in hot water for 30 minutes. Drain, reserving the liquid, and coarsely chop the mushrooms.

❖ Sauté shallots in oil and butter in a skillet until golden. Add herbs, salt and pepper. Cook for 2 minutes.

❖ Add reserved mushroom liquid. Bring to a simmer. Add the tomatoes. Simmer for 45 minutes or until sauce is thick and dark red.

Grilled Portobello Mushrooms

12 to 16 ounces portobello mushrooms
1/2 to 3/4 cup olive oil
1 teaspoon minced garlic
3 to 4 tablespoons balsamic vinegar
Salt and pepper to taste

❖ Place the mushrooms in a deep dish. Combine the remaining ingredients in a bowl. Pour over the mushrooms.

❖ Marinate for 6 hours to overnight.

❖ Drain the mushrooms and place on a preheated grill. Grill just until the mushrooms are light brown.

The Pasta Challenge

It seems that we in Rhode Island are always having a big food event and the public is invited to what is generally a fund raiser. One of the most interesting and well-attended events is the Keep Providence Beautiful Pasta Challenge held each fall in downtown Providence under the sponsorship of the Keep Providence Beautiful Committee.

A panel of food specialists and celebrities judge the event, except for the People's Choice Award, which is selected by votes of the general public. The following recipe, voted the best, is adapted from one submitted by the Union Station Brewery, 36 Exchange Terrace, Providence.

Chicken Penne

2 boneless skinless chicken breasts, cut into 2-inch pieces
2 tablespoons olive oil
Salt and pepper to taste

¹/₂ cup sliced mushrooms
¹/₂ cup finely chopped Tasso or Smithfield ham
1 teaspoon minced garlic
2 tablespoons white wine
1 egg yolk, lightly beaten
1 cup heavy cream
¹/₄ cup freshly grated Parmesan cheese
1 teaspoon unsalted butter
¹/₂ cup frozen peas
2 scallions, chopped
9 ounces penne, cooked

❖ Sauté the chicken in the olive oil in a large heavy skillet. Sprinkle with salt and pepper. Add mushrooms, ham and garlic. Sauté for several minutes. Add the wine. Cook until the juices are slightly reduced.

❖ Beat the egg yolk lightly with the cream. Stir into the skillet with the Parmesan cheese, butter, peas and scallions. Cook until thick rich sauce forms, stirring constantly.

❖ Add the penne and toss until coated.

❖ Yield: 4 to 6 servings.

MOM'S—It is really gravy, not sauce!

To truly appreciate this dish, we must give you a little background on the creator of MOM'S. If you have been in Rhode Island for any amount of time, or even if you are a non-Rhode Islander who reads a variety of things, you have probably heard of the Mayor of Providence, Vincent (Buddy) Cianci.

Mayor Cianci is a politician of the utmost, as well as a creative planner for the future of Providence. First elected in 1974, he has been reelected for a sixth time. The Mayor has been credited as the leading force in Providence, named as one of the nation's top cities of the year. Recently USA Today chose Providence as one of the United States' five Renaissance Cities. Cianci is convinced that Providence is the best.

The renaissance of the city includes the revitalization of the downtown area, which has moved three Providence rivers and created magnificent river walks and city waterviews complete with gondolas and a Fire and Water Spectacular. Major developments in the area include a convention center, hotel, and shopping mall.

When Buddy is not directing projects, meeting with constituents, or checking up on events such as the annual Keep Providence Beautiful Pasta Challenge, he is cooking up a storm in his own home. In 1994 he created a gravy (that is what it is called in Rhode Island—not sauce) that he introduced commercially as the Mayor's Own Marinara Sauce (MOM'S). The net proceeds go directly to the Mayor's Scholarship Fund to be awarded to deserving Providence high school students. Hundreds of thousands of dollars have been earned for this project from the sale of the sauce, which has received national attention. It is carried by gift shops and major supermarket chains in Rhode Island. See page 6 for other locations where it is available.

Mayor Cianci has this to say about great gravy and a great city. "A great gravy, like a great city, is a blend of many outstanding ingredients. It must be flavorful and a little bit flirtatious, tempting and terrific, combining all that is traditionally best with a creativity that embraces the new and the adventurous."

Pollo Fantasia con Vegetali

This "upscale" chicken dish was a team effort of Buddy, Chef Frank Terranova of Johnson & Wales University, and NBC's Channel 10 "Touch of Class" cooking show. It is quick and easy to prepare using, of course, the Mayor's Own Marinara Sauce.

1 (3-pound) frying chicken
1/4 cup olive oil
1 tablespoon minced fresh rosemary
8 ounces portobello mushrooms, sliced
1 large red onion, thinly sliced
1 cup cannellini beans, drained
2/3 cup white wine
1 1/2 cups Mayor's Own Marinara Sauce
1 (14-ounce) can artichoke hearts, rinsed, sliced
2 tablespoons chopped fresh basil
1 cup grated Parmesan cheese

❖ Cut the chicken into pieces. Heat the olive oil in a large deep skillet over medium heat.

❖ Add the chicken pieces. Cook for 5 minutes or until brown on one side.

❖ Sprinkle with the rosemary; turn the chicken over. Cook, covered, for 5 minutes.

❖ Add the mushrooms and onion. Cook, covered, for 5 minutes.

❖ Add the beans, wine and the Mayor's sauce. Cook, covered, for 5 minutes.

❖ Add the artichoke hearts. Cook, covered, for 3 to 4 minutes or until heated through.

❖ Sprinkle with the basil and cheese. Cook, covered, for 5 minutes longer. Serve immediately.

❖ Yield: 4 servings.

Marion King's Studio Casserole

This adaptation of Faraway Casserole, first made popular by Gloria Vanderbilt of the Newport Vanderbilts, is a great use of the Rhode Island Red Chicken developed in Little Compton, Rhode Island.

Marion's version is so easy. It can be made ahead of time for later baking, so she can spend the day in her studio.

1 cup sliced mushrooms
1 teaspoon olive oil
3 cups 2-inch cubes cooked chicken
1 cup sliced carrot rounds, cooked
4 medium potatoes, cut into 2-inch cubes
1 (16-ounce) package frozen peas and pearl
 onions, cooked
White Sauce
1 (6-ounce) package sour cream and onion
 potato chips, crushed

❖ Sauté the mushrooms in olive oil in a skillet.

❖ Layer the chicken, carrots, potatoes, peas and onions and sautéed mushrooms in a lightly greased 2^1/$_2$-quart casserole. Pour the White Sauce over the layers. Top with potato chips.

❖ Bake at 400 degrees for 15 to 20 minutes or until bubbly.

White Sauce

6 tablespoons butter
6 tablespoons flour
2 cups chicken stock
1^1/$_4$ cups milk
^{1}/$_4$ teaspoon each thyme, marjoram, minced
 parsley and tarragon

❖ Melt the butter in a medium saucepan. Blend in the flour. Cook for 2 minutes, stirring constantly. Stir in the chicken stock. Cook until thickened, stirring constantly.

❖ Blend in the milk gradually. Cook until thickened and smooth, stirring constantly. Add the seasonings and mix well.

Kirk's Spinach Flounder

On an especially hectic day, this South County speciality is just what you need—easy. For entertaining, it is colorful, can be made ahead, and is ready to pop into the oven when the guests arrive.

1¹/₂ pounds flounder or sole fillets
Garlic powder to taste
Cracked peppercorns to taste
1 cup white vermouth
Virgin olive oil to taste
1¹/₂ cups shredded white mild Cheddar cheese
3 or 4 scallions, minced
1 bunch fresh dill, thyme or other herbs of
  choice, snipped
1 (12-ounce) package fresh spinach
3 large tomatoes, sliced ¹/₂ inch thick

❖ Rinse the fillets with cold water. Place in a deep dish. Sprinkle with garlic powder and cracked pepper. Cover with the vermouth. Marinate in the refrigerator for 30 minutes or longer.

❖ Line a large baking dish with foil and spray with nonstick cooking spray. Arrange the fillets in the prepared dish. Drizzle with olive oil and sprinkle lightly with a small amount of the cheese and scallions. Add the herbs.

❖ Rinse the spinach well and discard the stems. Cover the fillets with a 2-inch-thick layer of the spinach leaves. (The spinach will cook down.)

❖ Sprinkle with a portion of the remaining cheese, covering the spinach completely. Arrange the tomato slices over the top, securing with large toothpicks. Drizzle with olive oil and sprinkle with cracked pepper. Cover with the remaining cheese and scallions.

❖ Bake at 375 degrees for 30 minutes or until the fish flakes easily.

Block Island is Known for its Swordfish

For years, Rhode Island waters, famous for the sportfishing tournaments held in Rhode Island Sound, have proved to be one of the finest areas for swordfish, notably, Block Island Swordfish. Whether or not the swordfish you get is from Block Island, this recipe—which was a winner in the State 4-H Favorite Foods Contest in the early 1950s—is outstanding. In recent years, the number of swordfish has been dwindling, and it no longer appears on many restaurant menus in an effort to allow the fish to recover to their former numbers. My adaptation of this winning recipe can also be made with mako shark or halibut steak. Be sure that the steaks are at least 2 inches thick.

Swordfish Westerly

2 pounds swordfish or halibut steaks
1/2 cup lemon juice
2 tablespoons melted butter
2 tablespoons flour
1 (6-ounce) can baby shrimp
1 cup milk
White pepper to taste
2 teaspoons chopped chives
1/2 cup sour cream

❖ Marinate the fish in the lemon juice in a covered container in the refrigerator overnight.

❖ Drain the fish, reserving the lemon juice. Broil the fish for 3 to 6 minutes on each side or until brown. Place in a lightly greased baking dish. (Fish may be prepared to this point and refrigerated for several hours.)

❖ Blend the butter and flour in a small saucepan. Cook for 3 to 4 minutes, stirring constantly.

❖ Drain the shrimp, reserving liquid. Stir the milk and shrimp liquid into the flour mixture.

50

Cook until thickened, stirring constantly. Stir in the shrimp, pepper, chives and sour cream. Cook until heated through. Blend in the reserved lemon juice for a sharper flavor if desired. Spoon the sauce over the broiled fish.

❖ Bake at 325 degrees for 15 to 20 minutes or until the fish is cooked through. Garnish with additional chives, fresh parsley, paprika and thin lemon slices. Serve immediately with roasted new potatoes, minted baby carrots and a green salad.

❖ Yield: 4 to 6 servings.

Herb Butter for Baked or Broiled Swordfish

❖ Combine $1/4$ cup finely chopped parsley, 1 tablespoon chopped dill or chives, 2 tablespoons lemon juice and $1/2$ cup melted butter in a small bowl. Bake or broil swordfish and use the herb butter during cooking or just before serving. This fish will be very moist.

Block Island Scalloped Lobster

1 cup hot milk
$1/2$ cup fresh bread crumbs
$1^1/2$ cups lobster chunks
1 egg, well beaten
$1/2$ teaspoon prepared mustard
1 teaspoon lemon juice
1 tablespoon melted butter
$1/4$ teaspoon salt
Pepper to taste
2 slices bread, buttered, diced

❖ Mix the milk and bread crumbs in a bowl.

❖ Add the lobster, egg, mustard, lemon juice, butter, salt and pepper and mix well. Spoon into buttered scallop shells.

❖ Process the diced bread in a food processor. Sprinkle over the lobster mixture.

❖ Bake at 400 degrees for 10 minutes. Serve with peas and a green salad.

❖ Yield: 4 servings.

A True Rhode Island Dish!

Probably the most asked-for recipe from out-of-staters is baked stuffed shrimp. Having grown up with them and knowing that shrimp is not a local shellfish, I had assumed that it was not a Rhode Island dish. Wrong! I researched all the references at my fingertips and, lo and behold, discovered that there was not a recipe for this Rhode Island specialty in cookbooks from other parts of the country or in general cookbooks. So, for cookbook collectors, local or out-of-state, Enjoy!

Rhode Island Baked Stuffed Shrimp

1 pound large shrimp, peeled, deveined
1 cup butter, melted
1/2 teaspoon Worcestershire sauce
2 tablespoons lemon juice
2 tablespoons minced fresh parsley
1/2 teaspoon garlic powder
Cayenne to taste
2 tablespoons bread crumbs
8 ounces Ritz crackers, crushed

❖ Split the shrimp to form a pocket. Rinse well, pat dry and place split side up on an ungreased baking sheet or in individual baking dishes.

❖ Mix the butter with the Worcestershire sauce, lemon juice, parsley, garlic powder, cayenne, bread crumbs and cracker crumbs in a saucepan Spoon the mixture into the shrimp cavities.

❖ Bake at 400 degrees for 15 minutes or until the stuffing is crusty and the shrimp are pink.

❖ Garnish with thin lemon slices and parsley. Serve immediately as an appetizer or as a main dish with additional melted butter on the side.

Gingerbread with Apples and Cream

Apple Slump

Margot's Cheesecake

Basic French Vanilla Ice Cream with Variations

Pompadour Pudding

Coffee Cream Pudding

Chef Wayne's Tiramisù

Coffee Milk

Grapenut Custard Pudding

Baked Doughnut Puffs

Lemon Cornmeal Biscotti

Erik's Soft Molasses Cookies

Quick Dessert Puffs

Phyllis' Prune Roll-Ups

Ethel's Strawberry-Rhubarb Conserve

South County Chocolate Pecan Pie

Squash Biscuits

Peggy's Irish Bread

Baked Zeppoles with Fillings

Winter Rumtoph

Spring Rumtoph

Rhode Island and the Molasses Trade

Molasses was an old-time Rhode Island ingredient. When it wasn't used for cooking, it was shipped by rum runners from the East Side of Providence as part of the slave trade agreements of the 1800s. I must say that this tasty dessert is a much better use for molasses. Apples of many varieties, especially the Rhode Island Greening, are readily available in Rhode Island. The higher hills of northwestern Rhode Island are home to many apple orchards, including many "pick your own" facilities.

Gingerbread with Apples and Cream

$1/3$ cup butter or margarine
$2/3$ cup boiling water
1 cup molasses
$2^1/4$ cups flour
$1^1/2$ teaspoons baking soda
$1/2$ teaspoon salt
1 teaspoon ground ginger
1 teaspoon ground cinnamon
$1/4$ teaspoon ground cloves
1 large apple, peeled, cored, finely chopped

❖ Mix the butter, boiling water and molasses in a bowl. Sift in the flour, baking soda, salt, ginger, cinnamon and cloves and mix vigorously.

❖ Spread the chopped apple in a greased 9-inch square baking pan. Pour the batter over the apple.

❖ Bake at 350 degrees for 35 to 40 minutes or until a toothpick inserted in the center comes out clean. Invert the gingerbread onto a serving plate.

❖ Serve hot or cold with vanilla ice cream, whipped cream or whipped topping.

❖ Yield: 9 or 10 servings.

Apple What?

In Massachusetts it's a grunt, but in Rhode Island it's a slump—tasty fruit and sugar stewed to a sauce and topped with a dumpling. Blueberries may be substituted for the apples.

Apple Slump

3 cups flour
4 teaspoons baking powder
2 tablespoons sugar
$1/4$ teaspoon salt
7 tablespoons shortening
1 cup milk
6 large cooking apples, peeled, cored, chopped
$1/2$ cup sugar
Cinnamon to taste
Sauce for Slump

❖ Sift the first 4 ingredients into a bowl. Cut in the shortening until crumbly. Add the milk and stir with a table knife until a soft dough forms.

❖ Place the apples in a heavy 4-quart saucepan. Add a small amount of water. Bring to a boil. Mix in $1/2$ cup sugar and cinnamon. Drop the dough by tablespoonfuls over the apples.

❖ Cook, covered, over low heat for 10 minutes; DO NOT PEEK. Dumplings should be cooked through inside and moist on the outside.

❖ Serve Slump hot topped with the warm Sauce.

Sauce for Slump

1 cup packed brown sugar
$1/2$ cup granulated sugar
$1^1/2$ tablespoons flour
1 cup hot water
1 tablespoon butter
1 tablespoon vinegar
1 teaspoon vanilla extract

❖ Combine the sugars, flour, water and butter in a heavy saucepan. Cook over medium heat until thickened, stirring constantly. Remove from the heat. Stir in the vinegar and vanilla.

Margot's Cheesecake

For a christening or confirmation party, this typical, festive dessert serves a crowd.

2 (3-ounce) packages ladyfingers (18 to 20 count)
16 ounces cream cheese, softened
2 cups heavy cream
$^1/_2$ to $^3/_4$ cup sugar
1$^1/_2$ teaspoons vanilla or almond extract
1 pint fresh strawberries, raspberries or
**   blueberries, or 1 (21-ounce) can fruit pie**
**   filling**
1 cup whipping cream, whipped

❖ Butter the bottom and side of an 8- or 9-inch springform pan. Line with parchment or waxed paper. Cover the bottom with ladyfingers and line the side with vertical ladyfingers.

❖ Combine the cream cheese, 2 cups cream, sugar and vanilla in a bowl and beat until smooth. Pour into the prepared springform pan. Freeze for 1 hour or longer.

❖ Loosen and remove the side of the springform pan. Remove the parchment or waxed paper carefully. Place on a serving plate.

❖ Spoon the fruit on top. Pipe the whipped cream in a decorative pattern on the top. Store in the refrigerator until serving time.

❖ Tie a 2- or 3-inch-wide satin ribbon around the ladyfingers just before serving.

57

Ice Cream

Think of a hot, sunny day in South County; you are on your way home from the beach and thinking, "Oh, for something refreshing!" You are probably thinking that Rhode Island's own Del's lemonade would hit the spot.

Well, I am thinking of a time before Del's. A time when families, believe it or not, used to take a Sunday drive together without a destination, but inevitably they would end at Maine's Ice Cream in Wakefield. It has been gone for years but my fond memories remain.

The following recipe was developed with 4-H member Sara Hutchings. We also discovered that the basic recipe could be used to make several different flavors, including an ice cream similar to the lemon ice cream that I remembered as Maine's.

Using egg substitute, 2% milk and instant pudding mix results in good flavor and texture but with a lower fat content than most ice creams. It only takes about 1½ hours to make this refreshing treat.

Basic French Vanilla Ice Cream

2 eggs or ½ cup egg substitute
¾ cup sugar
1 (3-ounce) package vanilla instant pudding mix (sugar-free is ok)
2 cups 2% milk
2 cups half-and-half
1½ teaspoons vanilla extract

❖ Beat the egg substitute in a mixer bowl until foamy. Add the sugar, pudding mix, milk, half-and-half and vanilla. Beat until the sugar and pudding mix dissolve and the mixture is smooth.

❖ Pour into a 2-quart ice cream freezer.

❖ Process following the manufacturer's instructions. Serve soft from the ice cream freezer or smooth the top, cover with waxed paper and place in your home freezer to harden and ripen.

Variations:

Lemon Ice Cream

❖ Follow the Basic recipe but reduce the sugar to ⅓ cup and add a 1-ounce container of Crystal Light lemonade powder.

Ginger Ice Cream

❖ Follow the Basic recipe and after 10 minutes of processing add ½ cup finely chopped candied ginger.

Coffee Ice Cream—a Rhode Island favorite

❖ Add 1 tablespoon instant coffee powder with the pudding mix.

Frozen Pudding Ice Cream

❖ Substitute rum extract for the vanilla and add ½ cup raisins and ½ cup coarsely chopped maraschino cherries.

Fruited Ice Cream

❖ Add 1 cup crushed fruit or berries 15 to 20 minutes before the ice cream is set and continue processing.

Fruit Swirl Ice Cream

❖ Swirl 1 cup crushed fruit or berries into the finished ice cream.

Ice Cream Sundaes

❖ Serve blueberries, strawberries, raspberries or peaches on the side. Sweeten the fruit if desired.

Where the Elite Used to Meet—Miss Dutton's Tearoom

With its wonderful dark paneled bar and black and white tile floor, Miss Dutton's Tearoom, Washington Street in Providence was the place to meet for a snack, lunch, or tea.

Shopgirls and bankers sat elbow to elbow at this Providence landmark. On Saturday afternoons, grandedames of the East Side with their best friends and their proper children dropped by for tea.

Flora E. Dutton, a Simmons College graduate in home economics, and a classmate became entrepreneurs of the restaurant in 1912. In time, she owned several lunch counters and cafeterias in the downtown area and managed seventy employees. She served her home-style, everything-made-from-scratch recipes using produce grown on her seventy-five acre farm in Swansea, Massachusetts.

Although Miss Dutton's Tearoom has been gone for years, fond memories remain—as well as some wonderful recipes. Two recipes we tested were both as delicious as we remembered them from the special trips when we went "down city."

Pompadour Pudding

A chocolate version of Floating Island, this and other dessert puddings are reminiscent of the first half of the century—light, tasty, and easy to make.

³/₄ cup sugar
¹/₄ cup cornstarch
¹/₈ teaspoon salt
3 egg yolks, well beaten
4 cups milk
1 teaspoon vanilla extract
2 ounces semisweet chocolate
³/₄ cup sugar
¹/₄ cup milk
3 egg whites

- ❖ Mix ³/₄ cup sugar with cornstarch and salt in a heavy saucepan. Beat the egg yolks until light and fluffy. Stir in 4 cups milk. Stir into the sugar mixture. Cook over medium heat until thickened, stirring constantly.

- ❖ Remove from heat. Blend in the vanilla. Pour into a 2-quart baking dish or 8 custard cups.

- ❖ Melt the chocolate in a double boiler or medium bowl over hot water. Add ³/₄ cup sugar and ¹/₄ cup milk and stir until well blended. Set the chocolate mixture aside.

- ❖ Beat the egg whites in a large mixer bowl until stiff peaks form. Fold in the chocolate mixture gently. Spread over the custard.

- ❖ Place the baking dish in a larger pan. Add hot water to the larger pan to a depth of 1 inch.

- ❖ Bake at 350 degrees for 30 minutes or until the topping develops cracks. Remove the baking dish from the hot water. Let stand until cool. Chill before serving.

- ❖ Yield: 8 servings.

Coffee Cream Pudding

Coffee is the flavor of choice in Rhode Island. This favorite old-time recipe is as delicious today as it was then.

2 tablespoons unflavored gelatin
¹/₂ cup cold water
2 cups hot coffee
¹/₃ cup sugar
1 cup heavy cream
Chopped nuts (optional)

- ❖ Soften the gelatin in the cold water. Add the hot coffee; stir until the gelatin dissolves completely. Heat if necessary. Add the sugar and stir until completely dissolved. Chill until partially set.

- ❖ Whip the cream until soft peaks form. Fold the whipped cream into the gelatin mixture gently. Spoon into a serving bowl, gelatin mold or individual custard cups. Chill until firm.

- ❖ Serve with a sprinkle of chopped nuts and additional whipped cream if desired.

The Best of Boston—In Rhode Island

It isn't often that you find a neighborhood restaurant that is as exciting as Il Piccolo's of Johnston. Tucked into a small shopping center in the heart of Johnston, not far from downtown Providence, is an eatery with Old World atmosphere that is worth the trip for tourists and natives.

Wayne and Monica Clark's first restaurant is known for the outstanding menu and cuisine that is matched by none in the area. Chef Wayne, formerly of Amsterdam's La Petite Auberge in Newport, and until recently chef at the Park Plaza Hotel in Boston, trained in France. Wayne changes Il Piccolo's menu frequently to utilize the offerings of his fish purveyor and seasonal favorites from his produce sources.

Il Piccolo is well known for its Italian food. Although the entrées such as pan roasted striped bass with caramelized onions, clams, herbs, and garlic are to die for, I urged him to share his own award-winning (Best of Boston '94) version of Tiramisù with us. He has cut the recipe in half for us, but it is still enough for a crowd—well worth the time and effort. For a smaller amount, half the recipe for a 9-inch square dish. You should know that this is the first time that he has given anyone the recipe!

The ladyfingers are not the usual spongecake type, but crispy and available at Italian specialty stores.

Chef Wayne's Tiramisù

3 pounds mascarpone cheese, at room temperature
1¹/₂ cups sugar
2 large eggs
2 cups heavy cream
1 cup dark rum
5 cups espresso or very strong coffee
50 Sandiardi ladyfingers
1 (28-ounce) can cling peaches
Cinnamon to taste

❖ Combine the cheese, sugar and eggs in a large mixer bowl. Beat at low speed for 3 minutes or until blended. Beat at high speed until smooth, scraping the side of bowl frequently. Set aside.

- ❖ Beat the cream until very thick. Do not overbeat or you will make butter. Fold into the cheese mixture gently. Set aside.

- ❖ Mix the rum and espresso in a bowl. Dip the ladyfingers, 3 at a time, into the espresso mixture and drain on paper towels.

- ❖ Spread a thin layer of the cheese mixture in a 9x18-inch dish. Arrange a layer of the dipped ladyfingers in the dish. Repeat the layers of cheese mixture and ladyfingers.

- ❖ End with a layer of the remaining cheese mixture applied carefully to avoid pulling ladyfinger pieces to the surface. (Wayne says that any leftover cookies are fair game.)

- ❖ Refrigerate the tiramisù overnight.

- ❖ Drain the peaches well and chill. Process the peaches in a food processor until puréed. Store in the refrigerator.

- ❖ Drizzle a small amount of the purée on each dessert plate. Add a portion of the tiramisù and sprinkle very lightly with cinnamon.

Coffee Plus

As noted earlier, the flavor of choice in Rhode Island is Coffee. In 1993, the legislature designated Rhode Island's official drink as:

Coffee Milk

- ❖ Stir whatever amount of coffee syrup you want into an 8-ounce glass of milk.

Variations:

- ❖ For a Coffee Shake—a slightly different twist—add 1/4 cup coffee syrup to an 8-ounce glass of milk; process in a blender until frothy.

- ❖ For Coffee Cabinet—the premier version—add 2 scoops of coffee ice cream and 1/4 cup coffee syrup to an 8-ounce glass of milk; process in a blender until thick and creamy. What is "coffee syrup"? Look for Eclipse or Autocrat brands in your supermarket.

Simple but Satisfying

In most family restaurants in Rhode Island the dessert menu is usually limited, but almost always includes Grapenut Pudding. I have been unable to track down its first appearance, but it has certainly become a mainstay of Rhode Island dessert menus.

For a tender custard, be sure that the oven is not too hot or the custard will curdle and the top toughen.

Grapenut Custard Pudding

4 eggs, beaten
4 cups whole milk
¼ cup sugar
1 teaspoon vanilla extract
½ cup Grapenuts
½ teaspoon nutmeg

❖ Beat the eggs, milk, sugar and vanilla together. Pour into a 1½-quart baking dish. Sprinkle with the Grapenuts and nutmeg.

❖ Place the baking dish in a large baking pan. Add water 1 inch deep to the large pan .

❖ Bake at 325 degrees for 35 minutes or until a knife inserted in the center comes out clean.

❖ Serve warm or cold, plain or with whipped cream or whipped topping.

Low-Calorie Grapenut Pudding

Not quite as rich as the original but still delicious.

Egg substitute to equal 4 eggs
4 cups skim milk
3 or 4 packets sugar substitute
1 teaspoon vanilla extract
⅓ cup Grapenuts
1 teaspoon nutmeg

❖ Beat the first 4 ingredients together. Pour into a 1½-quart baking dish. Sprinkle with Grapenuts and nutmeg.

❖ Bake in a waterbath as above. Serve warm or cold.

Is It Coffee Yet?

Most people take things around them for granted, I'm one of them. I yearn for a cup of "corfee" at different times. You can get coffee anytime of the day in Rhode Island. If you look around as you travel the highways and byways of our state, you'll see coffee and doughnut shops in very close proximity and motorists passing with the ever-present coffee mug either in hand or on the dashboard. Remember that Coffee Milk is our state drink. The next favorite is iced coffee, which we drink all year-round just as southerners drink iced tea.

And what is coffee without a doughnut? Or for those who prefer them, doughnut holes? Here is a recipe that mimics the best of both for taste but is lower in fat than either.

Baked Doughnut Puffs

2 tablespoons shortening
1/2 cup sugar
1 egg
2 cups flour
1 tablespoon baking powder
1/2 teaspoon each salt and nutmeg
1/2 cup milk
1/4 cup melted butter
3 tablespoons cinnamon-sugar

❖ Cream the shortening and 1/2 cup sugar in a bowl until very light and fluffy. Beat in the egg.

❖ Sift in flour, baking powder, salt and nutmeg alternately with milk, mixing well after each addition. Batter will be stiff. Drop by tablespoonfuls into greased miniature muffin cups.

❖ Bake at 400 degrees for 12 to 15 minutes or until golden brown.

❖ Dip tops of hot puffs into melted butter and then into the cinnamon-sugar.

Lemon Cornmeal Biscotti

Donna Lee shares this recipe that uses Rhode Island stone-ground white cornmeal, which can be purchased in most Rhode Island supermarkets (it's jonnycake meal). Substitute yellow cornmeal if you wish.

1 cup flour
1 cup stone-ground cornmeal
1/3 cup sugar
1/4 teaspoon salt
1 teaspoon baking powder
1/2 cup butter, softened
3/4 cup currants
2 teaspoons grated lemon zest
1 egg
1 egg yolk
1 teaspoon vanilla extract
1 tablespoon lemon juice

❖ Combine the flour, cornmeal, sugar, salt and baking powder in a food processor or bowl. Add the butter and process or work in with fingers until crumbly. Mix in the currants and lemon zest.

❖ Whisk the egg, egg yolk, vanilla and lemon juice together. Add to the flour mixture and mix well with a spoon.

❖ Turn onto a lightly floured surface. Knead several times. Divide into 2 portions. Shape each into a log and place on a foil-lined baking sheet. Flatten slightly.

❖ Bake at 350 degrees for 20 minutes. The logs will not brown.

❖ Remove from the oven. Cut into 1/3-inch-thick slices and place cut side down on the baking sheet.

❖ Bake at 350 degrees for 10 minutes longer. Remove the slices to a wire rack to cool completely.

❖ Store in a tightly covered container.

Erik's Soft Molasses Cookies

Cookies have always been favorites for snacking and school lunches. This old-time recipe from a Scituate grandmother doesn't take much time or effort. It will be fun for the kids to help—don't forget to have them help with the cleanup, too.

$^{1}/_{2}$ **cup shortening**
$^{1}/_{2}$ **cup sugar**
$^{1}/_{2}$ **cup molasses**
1 egg
2$^{1}/_{4}$ cups flour
1 teaspoon each ground ginger and cinnamon
$^{1}/_{4}$ **teaspoon salt**
6 tablespoons cold water
2 teaspoons baking soda
2 tablespoons hot water
$^{1}/_{2}$ **cup each raisins and chopped walnuts**

❖ Blend the shortening, sugar, molasses and egg in a bowl. Sift the flour, ginger, cinnamon and salt together. Add to the molasses mixture alternately with the cold water, mixing well after each addition. Dissolve the baking soda in the hot water. Stir into the flour mixture. Mix in the raisins and walnuts.

❖ Drop by tablespoonfuls 2 inches apart onto a greased cookie sheet.

❖ Bake at 350 degrees until golden brown. Cool on the cookie sheet for 1 to 2 minutes. Remove to a wire rack to cool completely.

❖ Yield: 1$^{1}/_{2}$ to 2 dozen.

Quick Dessert Puffs

❖ Prepare Puffs (page 16).

❖ Fill with your favorite pudding and top with a dollop of frosting or fill with your favorite ice cream and freeze until serving time. Serve plain or top with hot fudge or raspberry sauce.

Phyllis' Prune Roll-Ups

These popular cookies, a must for many Rhode Island families, are to be included for showers, family get-togethers, or the Christmas cookie plate.

$3/4$ **cup shortening**
1 cup sugar
2 eggs, beaten
$3^1/2$ **cups cake flour**
1 tablespoon baking powder
$1/2$ **teaspoon salt**
$1/3$ **cup milk**
1 teaspoon vanilla or almond extract
Prune Filling

❖ Cream the shortening and sugar in a large bowl. Add eggs and beat until fluffy.

❖ Sift the flour, baking powder and salt together. Add to the creamed mixture alternately with the milk and vanilla, mixing well after each addition. Chill for several minutes.

❖ Roll $1/8$ inch thick on a lightly floured surface. Spread with Prune Filling; roll as for jelly roll.

❖ Cut into slices and place cut side down on a nonstick cookie sheet.

❖ Bake at 400 degrees for 15 to 20 minutes or until light brown. Cool on cookie sheet for 1 to 2 minutes. Remove to a wire rack to cool completely. Frost if desired.

Prune Filling

2 tablespoons flour
1 cup sugar
1 cup chopped walnuts
$1/4$ **teaspoon salt**
2 cups chopped prunes, dried apricots or raisins
12 maraschino cherries, chopped
$1/2$ **cup raisins**
1 cup orange juice

❖ Mix the flour, sugar, walnuts, salt, prunes, cherries and raisins in a heavy saucepan.

❖ Cook over low heat until the consistency of marmalade, stirring frequently. Remove from heat. Stir in orange juice. Let stand until cool.

Ethel's Strawberry-Rhubarb Conserve

Adapted and updated from an old recipe of the Luther family of Scituate, this is delicious as an accompaniment to freshly baked bread or ice cream.

2^1/$_2$ cups chopped rhubarb
1 (8-ounce) can crushed pineapple
2 cups sugar
1 (3-ounce) package strawberry gelatin
2^1/$_2$ cups whole strawberries
1 cup broken walnuts

❖ Combine the rhubarb, undrained pineapple, sugar and gelatin powder in a saucepan. Bring to a boil, stirring constantly until the sugar and gelatin dissolve. Simmer for 5 minutes.

❖ Add the strawberries and walnuts. Return to the simmer.

❖ Ladle into hot sterilized freezer jars; seal. Let stand until cool. Store in the freezer.

❖ Yield: six (8-ounce) jars.

South County Chocolate Pecan Pie

1 cup each pecans and chocolate chips
1 tablespoon flour
4 eggs
^{3}/$_4$ cup sugar
^{1}/$_4$ cup packed brown sugar
^{1}/$_2$ cup melted butter
1 cup light corn syrup
1 teaspoon vanilla extract
1 tablespoon bourbon (optional)
1 unbaked (9- to 10-inch) pie shell

❖ Combine the pecans and chocolate chips in a bowl. Add the flour and toss until coated.

❖ Beat the eggs in a large bowl until light and fluffy. Add the sugars and butter and beat until well blended. Blend in the corn syrup, vanilla and bourbon. Add the pecan mixture and mix well. Pour into the pie shell.

❖ Bake at 350 degrees for 45 minutes or until a knife inserted near the center comes out clean.

Squash Biscuits

Remember the old Yankee saying, "waste not, want not." This old Rhode Island recipe was originally intended to use leftover winter squash. You will find that this very light yeast biscuit has a sweet, nutty flavor and stays fresh longer due to the addition of the squash.

1 envelope dry yeast
1/4 cup lukewarm water
1 cup milk
1/2 cup sugar
1 teaspoon salt
7 tablespoons margarine
1 cup mashed cooked winter squash
5 to 6 cups flour
Vegetable oil

❖ Dissolve yeast in lukewarm water.

❖ Heat the milk, sugar, salt and margarine just until the margarine melts. Blend the hot mixture into the squash in a large bowl. Cool to lukewarm. Blend in the dissolved yeast.

❖ Add 2 cups flour and beat until smooth. Mix in enough of the remaining flour to make a stiff, slightly sticky dough. Knead on a lightly floured surface for 5 minutes or until smooth and elastic. Place in a greased bowl, turning to coat surface. Let rise, covered, for 1 1/2 hours or until doubled in bulk.

❖ Knead several times on a lightly floured surface. Shape into rolls and arrange in a greased 9x13-inch baking pan. Brush lightly with vegetable oil. Let rise for 30 minutes or until almost doubled in bulk.

❖ Bake at 350 degrees for 30 to 35 minutes or until golden brown. Remove the rolls to a wire rack to cool.

❖ Yield: 2 dozen large or 4 dozen small rolls.

Only in Rhode Island

The most often heard phrase from TV talk shows to news items to groups at a coffee shop is "only in Rhode Island." Each year the state legislature calls a recess during mid-March to declare time for the joint celebration of St. Patrick's Day and St. Joseph's Day.

The Irish present their festive Irish breads and the patrons of St. Joseph, not to be outdone, bring out Zeppoles which can be either baked or deep-fried. Of course, both groups claim no calories.

Although similar to the original recipes, these are adaptations because the exact ingredients are not available here.

Peggy's Irish Bread

5 cups flour
1 teaspoon salt
5 teaspoons baking powder
3/4 cup sugar
1/2 cup margarine

4 to 6 tablespoons caraway seeds
1 1/2 cups raisins
2 eggs, beaten
1 1/2 cups buttermilk

❖ Combine the flour, salt, baking powder and sugar in a large bowl. Cut in the margarine until crumbly. Mix in the caraway seeds and raisins.

❖ Add the eggs and mix lightly with a fork. Add the buttermilk and mix well. Dough will be slightly sticky.

❖ Turn the dough onto a floured surface. Knead 10 times. Divide into 2 portions. Shape each into a round loaf and place on a greased baking sheet. Cut an X in the top of each loaf with a wet knife.

❖ Bake at 375 degrees for 45 to 60 minutes or until golden brown. Cool slightly before slicing.

Baked Zeppoles

St. Joseph is the patron saint of the family as well as those without a family, orphans, unwed mothers, the needy and homeless. St. Joseph's Day is celebrated on March 19th to thank the saint for helping them overcome difficulties during the past year.

Italians in Rhode Island have continued this tradition with zeppole filled with sweetened ricotta or custard cream. Neapolitans claim that the zeppole originated in Naples during the Middle Ages. A must for San Giuseppe's Day they can be found in most Italian bakeries and, of course, the Federal Hill section of Providence.

1 cup water
¹/₂ cup butter or margarine
1 cup flour
5 eggs
Custard Cream Filling or Ricotta Cream Filling
   (page 73)
Confectioners' sugar
Maraschino cherries

❖ Bring the water and butter to a boil in a heavy saucepan. Add the flour all at once and mix vigorously with a wooden spoon for 5 minutes or until the mixture forms a ball. The mixture should be fairly dry to make a light zeppole. Remove from the heat and let stand for 5 to 10 minutes.

❖ Add the eggs 1 at a time, beating well with a hand mixer after each addition.

❖ Fill a large pastry bag fitted with a ¹/₂-inch fluted tip with the mixture. Line a baking sheet with parchment paper. Pipe the batter into fat 4-inch circles to resemble doughnuts.

❖ Bake at 400 degrees for 40 to 50 minutes or until light brown and slightly crisp. Cool completely before filling.

❖ Split the zeppoles, fill with the filling of choice, replace the tops, sprinkle with confectioners' sugar and decorate with maraschino cherries.

Custard Cream Filling

1 cup sugar
$^1/_2$ cup flour
$^1/_2$ teaspoon salt
3 cups milk, scalded
2 eggs, beaten
3 tablespoons butter
$1^1/_2$ teaspoons vanilla extract

❖ Combine the sugar, flour and salt in a double boiler. Stir in the hot milk gradually. Cook over direct medium heat until thickened, stirring constantly.

❖ Stir a small amount of the hot mixture into the beaten eggs; stir the eggs into the hot mixture. Place over boiling water.

❖ Cook for 2 minutes, stirring constantly. Remove from the heat. Stir in the butter and vanilla. Cool completely.

Ricotta Cream Filling

❖ Combine 18 ounces sieved ricotta, $^1/_2$ cup sugar, 1 teaspoon vanilla and $^1/_4$ cup grated orange zest and beat well.

A wonderful mix of villagers from all parts of Italy came to live on FEDERAL HILL in the 1800s. This area has some of the best Italian bakeries, restaurants and markets anywhere. You haven't had REAL Italian bread unless you have tried Rhode Island's—a great Italian bread, crusty and crisp outside, moist inside.

Long gone are the pushcarts on Atwells Avenue used by vegetable and fruit vendors in colorful attire. When you visit the area, take time for a stroll, then dine at one of the family or upscale eateries. Or do what I enjoy doing: Buy a food item at each shop. It takes awhile, but it is fun—bread here, cheese and olives there, Italian cold cuts for an antipasto or ready to go, lasagna, pink vodka sauce and homemade ravioli, a bottle of wine and, of course, cannolinis or wandies. Recipes are included for many items, but to do it the easy way, Shop on the Hill!

A Visit from St. Nicholas

This famous poem, now best known as "'Twas the Night Before Christmas", was written in Newport, Rhode Island, by Clement Thomas Moore in 1822. James Van Allen read this classic to local children each year as part of the Christmas in Newport Festival.

"Visions of sugarplums danced in their heads" was my favorite part of the poem. I have interviewed many people to ask about their fond childhood Christmas memories. One of my questions is always, "What do you think sugarplums are?" Wouldn't you know it, each person has a different story.

When I was a young girl, going "down city" to Olneyville was not to be missed. Mall shopping will never replace the sights and sounds of Christmas: the birds flocking at dusk with their cries piping above the cathedral bells in the distance, the smells of the Planters peanut store—inescapable while dashing in the cold between Shepard's and the Outlet Company.

My father was a day-before-Christmas shopper. In late afternoon we would head for Olneyville for last-minute shopping in the 5 and 10 (cent store). Most important was the stop at the Providence Public Market and the Grand Central—then the closest thing to supermarket shopping. My father's idea of sugarplums was special sugar-dried fruit only available at Christmastime and expensive. My favorites were pineapple, pears, dates, cherries, and prunes.

Marion King's sugarplums were dates filled with peanut butter or almonds and rolled in sugar.

A more elegant "vision of sugarplums" were called bonbons by another friend who remembered going to a confectionery store to purchase delights filled with fondant or marzipan, covered with pastel-colored icing and decorated with flowers.

Another possibility is the traditional Rumtoph. I have an old advertising piece that includes a picture of the crock and a recipe. One family used a similar recipe served in a crystal compote.

A German friend reported, "Rumtoph meant the first fruits of spring. The crock was filled with fruits in season and added to during the year as fruit was removed. The grand finale was served on Christmas Eve and on through the holidays." The highlight was the children's squeals of delight as the first scoop of *fruit was taken from the crock.*

We are sure that the children went to bed willingly and with "hopes that St. Nicholas soon would be there."

Visions, yes, but different visions to be sure.

Winter Rumtoph

Winter rumtoph changes with the seasons and can be used to top off desserts the year around. Start yours now with chunks of fresh fruit, rum and sugar. Let the fruit mixture mellow to blend all the flavors, then add different fruits as they come into season.

3 medium fresh pears
3 medium oranges, peeled
1 cup seedless grapes
1 cup sugar
1 cup rum

❖ Combine the fruits in a crock. Stir in the sugar and the rum. Cover loosely with cheesecloth.

❖ Refrigerate for about 2 weeks before using.

❖ For every cup removed, add 1 cup of any fruit, $1/4$ cup sugar and $1/3$ cup rum. Serve plain or over ice cream.

Spring Rumtoph

The Germans say, "A rumtoph that begins in May will be ready for Christmas."

❖ Place a layer of fresh strawberries in a crock, cover with sugar and dark rum to cover by at least 1 inch. Cover the crock tightly. Check occasionally that fruit is covered with rum.

❖ Add fruits in season: unpitted cherries; peeled and quartered apricots and peaches; currants, lingonberries, blueberries and raspberries, plums, grapes, pears, pineapple. Layer the fruit, add sugar and rum to cover generously.

❖ It is traditional to let the family taste the rumtoph at Advent, but the fruit is eaten at Christmas with whipped cream, ice cream, pudding or a Melba.

Index

Index

Index

Cookbook Order Form

Stetson Laboratories, Inc.
P.O. Box 822
No. Scituate, RI 02857
(401) 647-3616

Photocopies accepted.

Your Order	Qty	Price	Total
It's Rhode Island—A Cookbook	_____	× $ 8.95 =	$ _____
Postage and handling	_____	× $ 3.00 =	$ _____
R.I. residents add (7% sales tax)	_____	× $ .65 =	$ _____
		Subtotal	$ _____
The Island Cookbook	_____	× $14.95 =	$ _____
Postage and handling	_____	× $ 3.50 =	$ _____
R.I. residents add (7% sales tax)	_____	× $ 1.05 =	$ _____
		Subtotal	$ _____
(Make checks payable to Stetson Laboratories, Inc.)		Total	$ _____

Sold To: (Please print)

Name _____

Address _____

City _____ State ____ Zip _____

Ship To: (If different address)

Name _____

Address _____

City _____ State ____ Zip _____

[   ] I would like a signed copy personalized for _____